SLENDER THREADS

A Conversation With Robert A. Johnson

ROBERT A. JOHNSON
with
J. PITTMAN MCGEHEE, SR., D.D.

CHIRON PUBLICATIONS • ASHEVILLE, NORTH CAROLINA

www.ChironPublications.com

Interior and cover design by Danijela Mijailovic
Printed primarily in the United States of America.

ISBN 978-1-68503-238-8 paperback
ISBN 978-1-68503-239-5 hardcover
ISBN 978-1-68503-240-1 electronic
ISBN 978-1-68503-241-8 limited edition paperback

Library of Congress Cataloging-in-Publication Data

Names: Johnson, Robert A., 1921-2018, interviewee. | McGehee, J. Pittman interviewer.

Title: Slender threads : a conversation with Robert A. Johnson / Robert A. Johnson with J. Pittman McGehee, Sr.

Description: Asheville, North Carolina : Chiron Publications, [2024] | Summary: "Robert A. Johnson was a Jungian analyst, an international bestselling author and lecturer. Robert's most famous books, He: Understanding Masculine Psychology, She: Understanding Feminine Psychology and We: Understanding the Psychology of Romantic Love, are beloved across the globe. Robert trained with C.G. Jung and his wife, Emma Jung, and attended the Jung Institute in Zurich, Switzerland with Joseph Campbell, among others. In spite of Robert's fascinating and accomplished life, he rarely sat for interviews. In 2002, Pittman McGehee, Jr. gathered a film crew of talented friends to film his father, Episcopal priest and Jungian analyst, J. Pittman McGehee, Sr. to interview Robert over the course of two days. The resulting film, Slender Threads, is a wide-ranging interview covering many topics relevant to today's world and has garnered quite an online following over the past 20 years. This book, Slender Threads, is based on the transcript of the interview, and includes an introduction by Pittman McGehee, Jr., Ph.D. as well as the original introduction to the film by J. Pittman McGehee, Sr. D.D"-- Provided by publisher.

Identifiers: LCCN 2024034620 (print) | LCCN 2024034621 (ebook) | ISBN 9781685032388 (paperback) | ISBN 9781685032395 (hardcover) | ISBN 9781685032418 (paperback) | ISBN 9781685034986 (hardcover) | ISBN 9781685032401 (electronic)

Subjects: LCSH: Johnson, Robert A., 1921-2018--Interviews. | Psychologists--United States--Interviews. | Jungian psychology.

Classification: LCC BF109.J64 A5 2024 (print) | LCC BF109.J64 (ebook) | DDC 150.19/54092--dc23/eng/20241024

LC record available at https://lccn.loc.gov/2024034620

LC ebook record available at https://lccn.loc.gov/2024034621

Robert A. Johnson
1921 - 2018

CONTENTS

INTRODUCTION

by Pittman McGehee, Jr., Ph.D.

"Our civilization has long since forgotten
how to think symbolically."
- C.G. Jung, *Symbols of Transformation* (1912/1952)

"A true myth teaches us the cure for the dilemma which
it portrays. The Grail myth makes a profound statement
of the nature of our present day ailment and then
prescribes its cure in very strange terms."
-Robert A. Johnson, *He* (1989)

Like many people, I would agree that C.G. Jung's writing can be intimidating at first. In Jung's great body of work, we are introduced to words like complex, archetype, collective unconscious, anima, animus, and theories about the human condition that can cause many of us to opt out too early. This is unfortunate, because it's with a better understanding of these words and ideas that we can find potentially transformative encouragement toward a more purposeful and meaningful life. Jung considered life to be "a pause between two great mysteries." Simply put, Jung's ideas help us live in and understand the challenging pause between a birth and death that we do not yet understand.

A man who finds life and relationships intimidating, can read about masculine psychology, feminine psychology, and the myth of romantic love and feel less alone and more capable in the world. A woman unsure of how she fits in a patriarchal culture, can inhabit this world of symbol and myth and find a long lost voice, or that she's been wearing, as Jung says, "shoes too small." Myth has bolstered the human experience for just this reason. If someone across the millennia has experienced what we are experiencing now, we feel less alone and might even find a guide along the way.

Robert A. Johnson had the unique gift of writing small and accessible books that brought Jung's ideas to people who might otherwise have decided Jung was not for them. Robert sold millions of books translated into many different languages because of this gift. Anyone who struggles to understand their feelings about masculinity can read a small accessible book called *He,* and through Parsifal have a deeper understanding of their own complicated feelings about masculinity. Anyone with a similarly complicated understanding of the feminine can read a book like *She,* and through Amor and Psyche, find greater awareness. In Robert's book *We,* Tristan and Iseult help us understand the complicated role of romantic love in our lives. Words and ideas that once seemed difficult to internalize become possibilities, and life can feel more manageable. Even broad ideas like meaning and purpose can become possible.

Much of my work as a psychologist has been in mindfulness and self-compassion. In the field of self-compassion, the concept of common humanity says that we are connected as human beings through our suffering. My friend, Kristin Neff, is a pioneer in the study of self-compassion and helped bring self-compassion into academic research. Kristin's research has found the great value in being compassionate with ourselves in our difficulties and struggles. Her work highlights three elements of self-compassion: mindfulness, self-kindness and common humanity. In order to be compassionate with ourselves, we need to be *mindful* and aware that we're struggling. Once we are mindful that we are suffering in some way, we bring *kindness* to ourselves, just as we would a friend struggling in a similar way. *Common humanity*, reminds us to experience our suffering within the context of what it is to be human. Typically, when we experience suffering we feel isolated, but through common humanity, we understand our connectedness to others, not through perfection, which doesn't exist, but through our imperfection. The fact that we suffer connects us.

Myth is common humanity. Reminding us who we are and that we're not alone. We are not alone on this human journey, but connected through slender threads, and every once in a while we are aware of them.

There are many threads that led to the film, *Slender Threads*, and therefore this book. The story of the film began in the early 1990s. I was living in Jackson, Wyoming and in those pre-Internet days frequented the local library to find books I could afford. The kind woman behind the desk saw a pattern and began to recommend books. One day she recommended *He*. It seemed like an odd name for a book, but on a recent camping trip my uncle had loaned me the Joseph Campbell companion and in that context, *He*'s subtitle, "masculine psychology" did make some sense. My librarian angel saw my smile as I bounced back through the library doors after reading *He* and recommended *She*. And then *We*. And then I was off. I talked about Robert and his books all the time, and some of those times people listened.

One of those who listened was my friend from the University of Texas, Mark Norby. Mark had just moved to Los Angeles and was deeply moved by Robert's book, *Owning your Own Shadow*. Mark had just started in the film world, and has since had a long career as a well-respected stunt performer and coordinator. We would often discuss Robert's work, and were amazed no one we knew had heard of him. So we hatched a plan to get him on tape.

I met Robb Bindler at Norby's wedding. Bindler had recently directed the highly regarded film, *Hands on a*

Hardbody, and had also found Robert's work. We laughed about how when we tell people about Robert Johnson, most say they also love the Delta blues. I filled Robb in on the plan that Norby and I had to get Robert on tape and Bindler was immediately interested. With Bindler on board, we now had a professional to tell us how and what to do.

In those pre-email/text days, I would have actual telephone conversations with my parents. In one of those phone calls, I told my Episcopal priest and Jungian analyst Dad that I had recently been reading Robert Johnson. The fact that he knew of Robert's work was predictable, but the fact that he actually knew Robert and had been analyzed by Robert was not. At that moment, the synchronicity of the slender threads was clear. Dad wrote Robert a letter in January of 2002 asking if he would be interested and available for a filmed interview.

Robert responded to Dad's letter in February, saying "Thank you for your warm and gracious letter! It put me in a good mood all day. Yes, I would enjoy doing a documentary with you." Robert attached a four leaf clover to the letter.

That summer, I flew from Austin to Los Angeles, met Norby and drove down to San Diego. Bindler met us there with his friend, Chapin Wilson, to help with sound. My Dad and brother, Jarrett, met us in San Diego and we spent two days filming Robert. Robert had asked that we film in short increments, as his leg would get tired and he needed to lie down. We honored that. Robert sent a letter to my Dad when he received the completed film on DVD, adding in the letter, "I thank you for your kindness and gentle ways in the taping process. You made it easy and a happy time." It warms my heart that Robert experienced an easy and happy time.

These slender threads came together to create the film and therefore this book. Robert was an incredible human being who lived in a deep and truly authentic way. Robert says in this book he believes in an ordered universe, which is "a nice polite way" of saying he believes in God. I believe in God because of people like Robert. Whatever God means to you and if God doesn't mean anything to you, I hope that his words and his way of understanding the world help you to be in the world in a more connected, meaningful way.

ACKNOWLEDGMENTS AND MORE THREADS

Thank you to the above threads. Your mark on this work is now well-documented. Without Norby and Bindler this film and book would not have happened. Bindler made the film. He filmed it, edited it, scored it. The world is better because of his work and the resulting film.

My Dad, Pittman McGehee, Sr. was the connective thread that made this film an actuality with his slender thread to Robert. When we were planning the interview, I had an idea of themes we needed to cover and reviewed them with Dad. We talked about how we would discuss these general themes in the interview. For instance, it was soon after 9/11 and we really wanted to document Robert's thoughts on the terrorist attacks. With this basic outline, my Dad then had a deep, meaningful, connected conversation over two days with his friend and mentor, Robert.

Another thread is my brother Jarrett. When I told him about my idea for this book, he was excited and supportive and helped with everything from the publishing contract to brain storming and editing. Without Jarrett this book would not have come to fruition.

Thank you also to Jim Hollis for pointing me in the direction of Chiron Publications and to Chiron for immediately getting the spirit of this project and for a shared interest in bringing more of Robert to the world.

Thank you to all who have sent letters or emails over the years expressing how meaningful this film is to you. The film *Slender Threads* has developed quite an online presence over the years, and in a world that appears to be falling apart at the seams, the fact that someone would spend over three hours listening to Dad and Robert in dialogue gives me great joy.

Pittman McGehee, Jr., Ph.D.
January, 2024

I.

Original Introduction to the Film, J. Pittman McGehee, Sr.

I'm Pittman McGehee, an Episcopal priest and diplomate Jungian analyst.

In Seminary, on a reading list in *Pastoral Theology*, there was a book by C.G. Jung, entitled, "The Undiscovered Self." I read it. It was life-changing for me.

As a young priest in a parish in Kansas City, I read in a neighboring parish bulletin that a Jungian analyst was coming to lecture on masculine psychology. I went.

I was so enamored with him and his subject that I literally followed him home, lived with him for a week, analyzed, learned. He became my first analyst and my longtime mentor.

For those of you who have not experienced Robert, you're in for a great experience of something sacred.

For those of you who know Robert through his lecturing or his books, you'll be reminded of what a great man this is.

For me, he's the holiest man I've ever met.

II.

THE LIVING MYTH

MCGEHEE: Jung used to ask his analysands, "What myth are you living?" Maybe that's where we start with this conversation.

From your autobiography and from our previous relationship and conversation, I know the myth of the wounded healer is a part of one of the myths you live.

JOHNSON: Yes, indeed. But more specifically, in the Grail myth, there's occasional reference to the old hermit who lives in the forest. And he doesn't turn up very often, but at critical moments, he and what he knows is needed. I resonate to that too.

MCGEHEE: What's interesting with those two archetypes of the Puer and the Senex, and as you started your life with all of that innocence of the Puer and the curiosity and the spirituality, and then the great injury of your life, accident in Portland when you had your near-death experience.

Was that your introduction to the Golden World?

JOHNSON: It was. The accident was when I was 11 years old and in the morning of that day I was a giddy kid and by midnight I was an old man and I vacillated back and forth between those two. And I haven't lost either one. One never gets over the Puer, just find your right place for it.

MCGEHEE: Balance seems to be a word in analytical psychology, but also in your lived life. Seeking a balance between the Puer and the Senex, between heaven and earth.

JOHNSON: The Puer lives over on the other side of my room here. Hermes sits and rules that side of the world. Buddha sits over here and he's the old, old ageless man. I want to live somewhere in between those.

MCGEHEE: So in Robert Johnson's psyche today at age 80 —

JOHNSON: 81, as of last week.

MCGEHEE: I stand corrected. At your age of 81, you're still integrating the Puer and Senex, the callow innocent fool and the wise old man. Both are present at the same time in this.

JOHNSON: Yes. They're both halves of a single archetype and life is not livable on any of these issues until one gets the two halves of a split archetype. There are dozens of them, at least conversant with each other.

MCGEHEE: Where Jung didn't exactly discover archetypes, it was he who named them and wove them into a part of the collective unconscious, the idea of ancient imprint and so forth.

Can you just say something about archetypal structure in psyche and how that's influenced your own development?

JOHNSON: Well, yes. It's basic to Jungian psychology and it's basic to all religion whether they know it or not. Jung borrowed the term "architect" I think from Greek mythology. Is it from Plato, I think?

MCGEHEE: The idea of the eidos.

JOHNSON: Yes. It's the building blocks of human structure. I think Jung has said, or he certainly would agree that everything that he, Jung, has said has been said many times in history. It must be said afresh for us and our current mentality.

So whether one is concerned with Greek mythology or the most primitive voodoo tales of Africa or whatever it is. One's working with the archetypes.

I have a table of treasures here. They're bits of things I have gathered from hither and yon. They're reminders to me of that great archetypal reservoir of energy and power and wisdom which every person carries within him. It would be a very wise man who could point out the current examples or language of the archetypal world.

MCGEHEE: Where would we see that?

JOHNSON: Everywhere. But it's so hard to see what is before your very face.

The movies present the archetypal world over and over again. I often don't like the form that they present, but it's there. It's interesting that the Tolkien myth is getting famous now. Maybe people are ready to listen.

And that's not precisely a modern presentation of the archetypal world, but it's a powerful one.

MCGEHEE: Well, Campbell, Joseph Campbell brought to the collective consciousness what we who study analytical psychology had known forever that the archetypes make themselves known in human lives but also in human literature, myths, fairy tales, legends.

JOHNSON: Yes. It is the psyche. We can't live without it.

I had a patient once who said, "All this church business, it's just complete rubbish. It's superseded. It's no good." I said, "Yeah, okay, but the old truths outside of time or outside of any date live all the time. Let's go to work and see what your archetypal structure is."

He was a scientist. Okay, dug into that. We had such a good time. He constructed a mythology or a theology, and energy was a primal source. Where did energy come from? Well, you have to start with energy. Energy doesn't have any history.

We went on and on. I was working very hard not to point out that he was recapitulating the whole psychic structure of mankind, giving it different names.

But he tumbled to that one day. He came in so excited. He said, "I have just rediscovered the religious life." I just renamed it. It was a profound effect on him. I don't know whether it transferred his allegiance from the old things to the new, or whether it disillusioned the new to him. I never quite found out. He died soon after.

III.

HE AND THE PARSIFAL MYTH

MCGEHEE: The first book you wrote was about an image of an archetype, the masculine: *He*. And you resonated so much to the Grail legend and chose that as the vehicle to introduce the masculine archetype. Can you say something to us about how that book evolved and what effect it's had both on you and on the reading public?

JOHNSON: Well, the Grail Myth touched me very deeply—beginning with childhood. I had a grandmother who read me the old Arthurian stories. She had to make them consistent with the Baptist Church, but that didn't spoil them.

I was thrilled with the dragons and the knights in the armor and the heroic quests and so forth. Slowly that myth evolved and matured in me. And I found out that I was living the Arthurian legends. I was Arthur.

Do you remember the wonderful moment when Arthur's been spirited away so he wouldn't be killed. And he's given to an old farmer who has ten children of his own and just tucked into the family. And only the old father and Merlin knew who Arthur was. So Merlin stays around and makes sure that Arthur is safe, and he tells all the ten kids plus Arthur the stories of knighthood. And he has them absolutely just on edge because the high point of his story is that it said that the new king, the true Arthur, has been born. He's somewhere. And the youngsters are beside themselves, and so they go out to find Arthur. And they look, and they look, and they keep pestering Merlin for information about where they would find Arthur. What would he be like? What would he look like and all the rest of it.

And the boy who is Arthur, but doesn't know it, most interested of all, he just can't sleep. He's so wound up over all of this. And finally, Merlin leads up to it and comes to the moment where he informs the boy who is nobody, you are Arthur.

Well, that's a good point in one's evolution, when these things, bit by bit, one at a time, turn into parts of oneself. And one can learn so much and get so much wisdom and information from the old myths of what it's like to be Arthur or to be Lancelot or be Guinevere or whoever it is and what one's up against and what to do and what not to do.

So finally I came around to lecturing about it. I was working with Jack Sanford at St. Paul's then. I did four lectures on the Arthurian Legends. Jack recorded the lectures without my knowing, transcribed them, tidied them up, sent them off to a little publisher who bought them. Then he told me what he had done.

MCGEHEE: That's how your writing career began?

JOHNSON: That's how it began. It would never have occurred to me to write a book. Harper bought the book from the little publishing house and Harper's taken me all over the world since.

MCGEHEE: Do you have any idea how many copies of *He* that you've sold?

JOHNSON: I think somewhere way back I heard that there were 250,000 copies out, and we got past the two million mark of all of my books.

MCGEHEE: You sold over two million books.

JOHNSON: For a shy guy, I've gotten around.

MCGEHEE: So the Arthurian legend, and I know you had, in addition to us, owning the king and the warrior in each of us and coming to the recognition that those stories are about us and those are archetypal images that each of us carry. You were particularly fascinated by Parsifal.

JOHNSON: Well, I'm such a good Parsifal.

When I was in Zürich, I took a room in a private house, got to be friends with the owner of the house, who was a translator. He and his wife would invite me down for tea occasionally. They were discussing the translation of Portuguese into Polish or something or another, which is beyond me.

One day they broached it, "Robert, we're tired of calling you Robert. Can we give you another name?" "Well, all right. What do you want to call me?" "Well, we want to call you Parsifal." I thought that was odd, but all right, so they began calling me Parsifal.

Mrs. Jung was lecturing at the Institute on the Grail Myth, which was her child. Dr. Jung had agreed never to write or publish anything on the Grail Myth because that was hers. But she announced the word "Parsifal" means innocent fool.

So next time I had tea with my landlord, I said, "I bet you don't know what Parsifal means." Oh, yes, we know.

MCGEHEE: You personified that for them.

JOHNSON: Yeah, they knew. They recognized one.

IV.

INTRODUCTION TO THE GOLDEN WORLD

MCGEHEE: What's the relationship between the Parsifal legend of coming into the castle too soon and not being able to ask the question, and your own golden world experience as an 11-year-old boy in a near-death experience.

JOHNSON: Absolutely parallel. I had written my book and bravely announced that one has a second chance at the Grail Castle sometime in midlife if he has lived his life and if he is capable and if quite a few things. But it hadn't happened to me. So I got to India, I think. What was I, 54 years old? A little bit late for middle age, but I've been late for everything.

MCGEHEE: Psyche has its own time.

JOHNSON: Yes.

Forgive, I'll talk a little bit about that because it's important to me.

I go on to India. And I'm not a very brave person. It's not like me to take off alone on some big venture halfway around the world. So I bought a ticket. My friends shook their head. What's Robert going to do now?

Flew for twenty-four hours, thirteen and a half time zones, dog tired. Arrive in India about 3 a.m. My luggage is lost. I'm the last one out. A mob of taxi drivers who hadn't gotten the fare yet, maybe 20 of them and they started fighting over me. I didn't know what to do. So I had some kind of instinct of what to do. So I chose one of them, told him to take me to a western style hotel.

Off he went. Arrived at the hotel, maybe 6 a.m. Yes, they had a room, tenth floor, up we go. Bellboy takes me to my room and opens up the drapes and it's just dawn. So I give him his tip. Think there's nothing in this world that I want more than just to fall into bed and sleep for about 36 hours.

But just about to that time, the sun was beginning to rise, and here was the horizon of old Delhi: mosques, minarets, castles, towers. I was absolutely enchanted. And just as the sun came up, the same gold in the world that had struck me dumb in my childhood, near-death experience of the accident, burst out in all of its glory again and justified my audacious observation that you have a second chance at the Golden World. That went away again.

To pursue that theme, it reappears periodically for me, somewhat considerably reduced form, it doesn't just flatten me out. But that experience has the effect of making anything else seem very tame or inadequate for one, and that's the great danger of it.

These young guys who turn up at my door these days, they're all Parsifals. They've all been half-blinded by some kind of an insight of beauty or love or the numinous or God knows what. And nothing else works for them, nothing else is sweet or nothing else is worth it. And he'll come and sit in my chair here and say, "But what shall I do? There's nothing I want to do. There's nothing worth it. We're all going to hell in a basket. What shall I do?"

Well, hang on until you've matured enough so that the golden world will come and have a try again. And if you're still there, you're still sane, you haven't committed suicide, then maybe you can hold it that time. But that's thin fare for somebody who's suffering and hurting like hell, lonely as hell. But that's the story.

MCGEHEE: From the beginning of the car wreck in Portland that pinned you against the wall and you lost a leg and the hospital story of the bleeding leg that a wise competent nurse saved your life.

JOHNSON: Yes. They got me to the hospital and the main artery had been severed in the back of my knee. And they sutured that up and put me in a cast. And about midnight the artery broke loose, and in a cast, nobody noticed. I was bleeding to death. And that's what took me within an eighth of an inch of death itself.

But I found out that the nothingness, the blackness, the total disaster was also the ecstatic world. But that's a terrible thing to land on an 11-year-old. A nurse found the blood seeping through the cast and they whisked me off to the surgery and dragged me back again against my will. I'd seen something. I wasn't going to let loose of it.

MCGEHEE: Jung tells a similar story when he had his heart attack and was instructed by someone that he had to come back to the world of boxes.

JOHNSON: (Laughs) Typical.

MCGEHEE: He didn't want to come back either.

JOHNSON: No.

MCGEHEE: Why do you think you came back Robert? What were you brought back for?

JOHNSON: They dragged me back. My problem has never been the inner world or the next world. My problem has been whether I would buy this world. I dragged my feet on that one for years and years.

It was Fritz Kunkel who convinced me to live because I needed human faculties to see the things that I treasured so much.

MCGEHEE: Kunkel was your first analyst.

JOHNSON: That's right. Jack Sanford's first analyst too. We never met at Kunkel's front door, but uh…

MCGEHEE: But you were seeing him at the same time?

JOHNSON: Yes.

MCGEHEE: I know Jack's written a book on Kunkel.

JOHNSON: Yes. And Jung proceeded to teach me some more about—how does somebody who's blinded by the inner world and in serious danger from it. It can go into a psychosis, or it's the stuff of suicide, or it's the stuff of addiction. I think most addictions come from somebody trying to drown out that which is too good to stand.

MCGEHEE: Jung's credited with beginning, influencing the Alcoholics Anonymous program by saying that alcoholics are very spiritual people, they just have the wrong spirits. And that's what you're saying.

JOHNSON: Yes. I can shock people severely by saying your neurosis is a religious experience that you're not taking correctly. Now don't get rid of it, but mature it. One's neurosis is the language of God always. Most people walk out when they hear that. They want somebody that'll cure them.

MCGEHEE: Neurosis is suffering that hasn't found its meaning, said Jung. So the world's been a problem for you, the outer world.

JOHNSON: That's right. Well, it's not a very attractive place.

JOHNSON: It's going downhill more and more I fear, but men have been saying that for centuries.

MCGEHEE: Maybe that's the old man's role.

JOHNSON: I spent a lot of time with Krishnamurti early in my life. And he was the archetypal old man, wise old man. And that's all he knew. He didn't know anything else. And the gulf between us was too great, and no communication took place over that gulf.

My memory of Krishnamurti is that I aged. I don't know what it was, 22 or something. Sitting in my chair, desperately needing a father, desperately needing teaching, desperately needing to belong somewhere. And this beautiful old man, sitting in his chair, he would get exasperated, poor man. He would get wound up in that high-pitched tenor voice, if you say, "Look, is it too much? Can't you understand? All you have to do is to be aware. Is that too much?"

Well, of course it's too much. For years I thought I was just too stupid to understand and there are lots of other people around shaking their heads. Yes, yes, yes. And I slowly found out that nobody else could climb that vertical wall either. Eastern teachers tend to do that to Westerners. And no matter how valid the Eastern teacher is, he's likely to bring his student to a vertical granite cliff and say, "Climb." And a westerner can't do it.

So I was getting worse and worse, more and more lonely, and my neurosis chewing at me. So I left. A friend bundled me up, took me to Fritz Kunkel. He was a good therapist. He began where I was and I took hold of him.

V.

SLENDER THREADS TO ZÜRICH

MCGEHEE: Is that your first introduction to Jung?

JOHNSON: Yes. Well, I had been reading some Jung, though there wasn't very much in English and no von Franz to write intelligibly for us. I think there was only one book in English from Jung's *Secret of the Golden Flower*, which is about as indigestible as Krishnamurti was.

MCGEHEE: Well we are beginning to discover the threads you talk about.

JOHNSON: Yes, yes.

MCGEHEE: And how important those connecting threads are to one's tapestry...

JOHNSON: Oh, I've lived on slender threads and they have been slender at times, I tell you. They worked somehow.

I remember when I decided to leave Krishnamurti, I saw what was going on. I saw that he was telling me something that I intuitively knew was true, but was not within my grasp. Not possible.

I remember the day I was in an orange grove, and I remember the slant of the sunshine. And I swore if I ever got old and wise, very unlikely, I would never do that to people. I remember carefully when young people come, don't blast them with something that they're already choking on.

MCGEHEE: So how did you get from Kunkel and your first analytic work to Zürich?

JOHNSON: That required several slender threads, smaller than spiderwebs. My one criticism of Fritz Kunkel was that he didn't warn or protect me from inflation. He never spoke of such a thing. I immediately began feeling better and my dreams were flowing and I was getting excited and energy was flowing in my bloodstream. So I promptly inflated it. Oh, I'm a really great guy, you know.

MCGEHEE: I now know something.

JOHNSON: Yes. I'm still embarrassed if I meet somebody, rarer these days, who knew me in those days because I was a complete jackass. A happy one.

So I decided I've always wanted to go to Europe. I'm going to Europe. 1948, tickets across the Atlantic were just almost impossible. Most of the shipping in the world was at the bottom of the sea. But I found a ticket on a freighter, flew to New York, got on the freighter.

There was a war scare there then. It looked as if Russia might just walk across Europe to the Atlantic Ocean. I understand later they could have. Somehow they didn't. But there was a scare, and most of the people on the ship just got off. They delayed the sailing for two or three days. Very few people left on the freighter. It was a converted troop transport, not converted in any sense. So I was sitting on the hatch cover of a converted troop transport, preening myself and patting myself on the back, and life's good. I'm going to Europe. Well, whistles blew and ropes were tossed off and a gangplank was hoisted aboard. Then when the ship was just too far from the wharf for me to jump. My inflation collapsed. It collapsed like a balloon that had been bricked.

MCGEHEE: All in a moment.

JOHNSON In microseconds. I'll never forget. I was thrown into just a complete panic. Inflation's do that.

MCGEHEE: Psyche compensates.

JOHNSON: I went from being absolutely nobody. I remember a dream I had when I was working with Dr. Kunkel that I was such a despicable person that I lived in the sewers of Los Angeles. I was managing okay, all alone and somehow functioning. I was walking along and somebody flushed a toilet in the YMCA right down on my head. I took the dream to Fritz Kunkel and I said, Look, you have to tell me there's no hope. With a dream like that, what hope can you have? I think I was in tears. And he says, "On the contrary, you were baptized. Now you will get better." So without some help, and I probably would have done it anyway, but I went from there to sky high. I know a way now and I'm cured and I'm happy and I'm somebody. I went to as dangerous a state on the opposite side of the teeter-totter.

MCGEHEE: So you were deflated on the boat to Europe.

JOHNSON: Yes, but that too low led to too high, which I think is inevitable for most people. Brains would help, but not always. And I was so scared I couldn't function. I remember not eating for ten days on the crossing. I said

I was seasick, but I wasn't. What am I going to do? I don't have much money. Ships going to France. I can't speak any French. What am I going to do? And I barely pulled myself together in ten days at sea and began to function. So slender threads like that were taking care of me, and still are. They're a little bit thicker now, but not much.

MCGEHEE: I'm fascinated by the fact that you got to Zürich in the most unpredictable and unexpected way.

JOHNSON: Another slender thread. I made friends with a young fellow in somewhat the same predicament as myself on the ship. So we went to Strasbourg for a music festival. It was a wonderful time. A delicious month of music. France's first effort to pull itself together in the way of a festival after World War II. It's time to go home then. At least my finances said it was time to go home. But I got an idea in my head that look, I'm only three hours from Switzerland, and I can't give up Switzerland when it's only three hours away. So we got on a train to go to Switzerland, just set foot in Switzerland. He knew somebody in Zürich, so we went to see them. There were good friends of Jolande Jacobi, one of the principal analysts of the Jung society in Zürich.

Jolande Jacobi is an extraordinary person. She's a Hungarian Jewess, wildly extroverted. It was she who had pulled the institute together. And Jung said, "That's not the way to do it. If you want to be stupid enough to set up an institute, you go ahead, but I'm not going to set foot in it." So she was plowing ahead.

Well, the friends insisted that I go and meet Dr. Jacobi, for what reason? I don't remember, or maybe there was no reason. So I went immediately to Dr. Jacobi's consulting room. And she did a pretty good job of kidnapping me. Before I knew what had happened, I was enrolled in the Jung Institute.

Maybe it's ungraceful of me, but I often thought she was just beating the streets to get enough people into the Institute to get it functioning.

MCGEHEE: But it was a thread.

JOHNSON: Yeah. I began analysis with her. I've analyzed with six different people in my lifetime, and she was the most unsuitable of all of them. I've had people laugh at me when I said that I analyzed with Dr. Jacobi, "Well, how did you survive it?" I didn't.

The classes had started and I was liking what I was hearing. I scratched around and got enough money too, for the month at least. I had a very big dream, just a huge great archetypal dream. One of these nodal points in one's life that are so important if one can hear them, and I think it frightened her. But she announced that that's an old man's dream. We're not going to talk about that.

Well, the hell with you, so I walked out. She used to conduct her analytical hour pacing. She'd walk. Like watching a ping pong tennis match. But I had to strengthen the understanding to get out of that. This is, this is not correct for me.

So I went to Mrs. Jung, who was lecturing on the Grail myth at the Institute. I asked if I could continue my work with her. I took my big dream to her. She didn't say anything either, but not in the sense of dismissing it.

So she talked the dream over with Dr. Jung that night, and he phoned the school the next day. Talked to me on the phone. He said, "You get out here. I want to talk *at* you." I remember he said, "at." And that's about what he did. First meeting with him, I didn't see him often, I stayed with Mrs. Jung, but the occasional talk with Dr. Jung. He was just in the midst of his last books then. Didn't want to spend time with school or many patients, but he told me what the dream meant.

MCGEHEE: Was this the hooded snake dream or what?

JOHNSON: Not the hooded snake, but yeah, you're thinking the right one, yes. He made it clear he didn't want me to interrupt him. He told me what the dream was about. He told me who I was, what it was good for, what it was not good for. I understood. I knew what he said was correct. But again, I wasn't strong enough or mature enough to take it. So, as you put it, I disobeyed him numerous times along the way, but he was right in every case.

MCGEHEE: He admonished you...

JOHNSON: He told me to put my whole attention and hopes on the inner world and that it would take care of me. But I was not to spend energy in the outer world. I didn't have to get somewhere. Even if I never accomplished anything in my life, I would make my contribution to the world in that manner, in an interior way. Not to marry. He said over and over again, "Trust the inner world and it will take care of you." He found half a dozen different languages to say that.

I've worked on that dream all the rest of my life. And it was 35 years later that I had a sequel which finished the dream or took it out of the cliffhanger which it stopped with and brought it to a conclusion. I wish so much Dr. Jung could have heard the sequel.

MCGEHEE: What was he like? What was it like for you experiencing C.G. Jung?

JOHNSON: The first time I'd ever seen him. There's this big man. He wasn't as old as I am now, but close to it. This is 1948. Big man, big voice, gruff man. He was famous for being hard on people. He wasn't on me. He knew I couldn't take that. He was immensely kind to me. And his greatest gift to me was that not only did he speak English with me, I didn't know German, but he spoke my typology with me.

He spoke my introverted feeling and character to me. Used language which would be appropriate for that, and treated me in that manner. It was only later when I saw him in a public situation that I found out that he himself was quite a different person from that. I resented that. I was just basking in the fact that here's somebody just like me, only older, wiser, more intelligent, but exactly like me, of somebody I can identify with. But when I saw him in public, I saw that he was somebody quite different. It took me some time to find out that he had been giving me the gift of containing his own personality to meet mine. I made another vow that insofar as I could do such a thing, I would do that for other people.

It's a fine art. I never learned how to pace before somebody. That's not within my problems.

MCGEHEE: So a form of empathy is the ability to access your own type and function to fit with the person that Psyche has brought to you.

JOHNSON: Yes. I have the experience of various people talking about me. Come and report utterly different stories and want to know which is correct.

There's a story about Jung who was at a party somewhere in America, and two people came to him. They'd both been analyzed by him. And she said, "Isn't it wonderful? And won't make a move without consulting dreams." And he said, "What are you talking about? We never talked about a dream the whole time we were together." So they set to quarreling.

They went to Dr. Jung and said, "Now, what about this?" No, I've got it wrong. They wrote to him, it wasn't a party. In due time he wrote back and he said, "Dear Madam and dear sir, you are different people. Sincerely yours, C.G. Jung."

VI.

SHE AND THE PSYCHE/EROS MYTH

MCGEHEE: When you wrote *She*, did you plan the trilogy of *He*, *She* and *We* or did they evolve?

JOHNSON: They evolved and it was the publisher who named them to my embarrassment.

MCGEHEE: You chose the Psyche/Eros myth for *She*.

JOHNSON: Yes.

MCGEHEE: And why so?

JOHNSON: To me it's the most intelligible and the most coherent of the feminine stories that could parallel the Grail myth for masculinity.

I'm embarrassed at probing into feminine psychology like that, but if I stayed close to the myth, I felt reasonably safe. Feminine psychology is very different from masculine.

Not many men are coherent in that language. And not very many women are vocal about it. Women's mysteries tend to stay mysteries.

I'll tell you a funny story on that score. I'm good friends with Alan Jones at Grace Cathedral in San Francisco. His mother-in-law was Madeline L'Engle, who has published a great many books, and was held in high esteem. Madeline L'Engle was part of a conference in North Carolina at Kanuga where Journey Into Wholeness was also holding forth. I tried to find Madeline L'Engle and introduce myself. I couldn't find her. I was at lunch, crowded cafeteria, balancing a tray in my hands, trying to keep my balance, which is not easy for me. People can give me a moderate-sized push and I'm in bad trouble. In the midst of all of this, a little very short, old woman dressed in an old-fashioned manner came up to me.

"You're Robert, aren't you?"

"Yes."

"I hear you don't like women priests."

I said, "That's true. I would agree to a priestess, but I don't like women priests."

"Oh, and what would a priestess do that a priest doesn't?"

And here I am, tottering around, not prepared for this in the least. I said, "Well, I don't know. The tradition has been broken, but I'm sure she would do it at midnight in the crypt."

That offended her so much, she turned around and walked off, and never seen her again.

MCGEHEE: So we're back with the archetypes and the masculine and the feminine. Jung chose the Latin for soul, anima and animus to talk about those contra-sexual archetypes.

JOHNSON: Yes. They're so important to us now. One can't make her way through the modern world without understanding anima and animus. The man with his feminine side, the anima, ruling so much of his personality, the woman with the animus, her masculine side down underneath, ruling so much of her personality. And the modern world is doing very badly with these. That's so much of the chaos in marriages these days.

MCGEHEE: So as we think about the archetypes of masculine and feminine and their images of anima and animus, souls. Much of falling in love is the projection of that archetype onto a living human being. Very dangerous territory.

JOHNSON: Very dangerous. That's what my book "We" is about.

If I could naively wish small things for a modern man, one of them would be to differentiate between masculine and male, and female and feminine. People can't tell the difference. And the feminine side of me doesn't fit onto a female. One automatically presumes that that's so.

If something wells up in me, feeling nature and soft and tender and feminine, we take it naively to think that there's a woman who will carry that for me. That doesn't work.

If I'm going to relate to a woman, I must relate to her as a woman, not as my feminine, vice versa with a woman.

Our age hasn't learned this and is putting up a huge resistance to learning it. Well, a fairy tale, finding the perfect woman and live happily ever after would come crashing down.

MCGEHEE: What happens when the projection collapses?

JOHNSON: Disillusionment. Which is a noble word, but not a happy one.

MCGEHEE: So the state of falling in love, no thing is just one thing, but one of the dimensions of falling in love is the projection of the archetypal energy onto another human being which will eventually collapse.

JOHNSON: No human being can carry that. Neither one of the people involved.

Yet people keep trying. Second time, fifth time, find somebody who will carry that expectation.

That's a fairly recent addition or error in the Western psyche. Romanticism. The putting of an archetypal structure on a human being. And it doesn't exist in India, or the so-called third world. Indians don't fall in love. Westernized Indians do after they see our movies, and by the time they get a TV.

To fall in love with somebody is to fall into the religious dimensions of one's psyche, and it's absolutely real and tremendously powerful. But one must be keenly aware of levels if one is to survive it.

You ask some human being person to carry that for you, and he, she can't. You'll try, but it's not possible to be a living, walking archetype for somebody else.

People put the archetype of the Savior on the priest, and if he can stay sufficiently impersonal and out of reach, okay, maybe they can hold up under that. But nobody can live up to that archetype. The Catholic Church is discovering that now. The errors or the humanness or the fallibility of the people preached to who committed some indiscretion or another. There's a big uproar over it. The Catholic Church at least is still trying to hold up to the old laws that the priest is celibate and he is not involved in the human passions. A great idea.

People sometimes try to make a saint out of me. If I can escape fast enough, they can keep it going so long as I'm absent. I think it might be a stage that one goes through, wakes one up to the presence of that archetype, but one must go past the projection of it. Most people don't welcome that.

MCGEHEE: It's pretty tempting to inhale that ether though, for human beings who are recipients of projections of others. How have you handled that through the years when people are projecting sainthood onto you?

JOHNSON: Well, first off, I don't ask for it. I don't welcome it. Some people do. They live on it. They cultivate a persona like that.

And if there's a discussion about it, I will say just what we're saying now that, okay, the projection is true, but it's not true on the level that one is trying to make it true.

Forgive please, but I know two people. I know you, and I know Father McGehee. They're different. I hear about Father (McGehee), the legends and you practically walk on water. Well, that's true. Where it is true. It is true in the archetypal world. It's true in the timeless world. But you're a little heavy to walk on water, in fact.

Okay, I know the difference between the two. But if I fall in love with somebody, that's a hard one.

MCGEHEE: I remember you in a lecture saying, asking the question: "Could Beatrice ever have become Mrs. Dante?"

JOHNSON: (Laughter) I had a patient once, a minister, and he had fallen in love with his secretary. I did a quick course in differentiating of levels with him, and he understood. A man of high integrity.

Anyway I went out to the waiting room to get my patient, and there was a strange woman there, not the man I was expecting. She announced that she was Mrs. and so on and so forth. So I took her into the consulting room, and she sat down and she said, I have come to announce to you that I am not willing to be Mrs. Dante, who he and I had been discussing in these terms. Well, by the end of the hour, I had convinced her that she was Mrs. Dante. She was the man's wife, three children. She was not "le fom in spiritaries," as the French would call it. She was an intelligent and person of high integrity. So we got some things settled on appropriate levels. They also survived.

MCGEHEE: It's a powerful projection.

JOHNSON: Probably the most powerful that a modern ever experiences. And it is his religious life. What he does with it makes or breaks his connection with the interior world.

Jung defied the anima of the feminine side of the man, which he so handily puts on the girl as the intermediary between himself and the interior world.

We've somehow got it skewed around and trying to make her the intermediary between oneself and the outer world.

Men go around trying to house their anima somewhere and generally make donkeys of themselves doing it.

MCGEHEE: They only have human beings to project onto and nobody can carry that.

JOHNSON: Well, people try. Movies are still busy out there. All you have to do for a best seller is boy meets girl and live happily ever after.

There's a curious thing going on which nobody's understanding very well, me included: the dilemma of the gay world. I'm tentatively of the conclusion that when a boy falls in love with a boy, he (has) put his anima on that boy. He acts like it and the same purple haze is in the air.

I don't know why one should put the anima, which is feminine, but not necessarily female, onto a male, but it seems to happen.

MCGEHEE: The very important distinction that you've made and we need to continue to make between the archetype and the stereotype. So many women, when I'm lecturing about the country, will come up all full of their animus angry at me for stereotyping women, when in fact I'm talking about the feminine, which has been wounded in men and women as well by the patriarchy. And that distinction is hard to hold.

JOHNSON: People can't hear. They won't hear.

Marian Woodman and I were lecturing together. And she said, "Robert, I'm going to risk something and I want you to back me up." She said, "I'm going to tell this audience," which is 90 percent women, "that the worst form of the patriarchy they ever run into is their own animus, their own interior masculinity." And I said, "Well, I'm glad it's you saying it." They tar and feather me if I said it.

So the afternoon went on and the hall was absolutely full. It was hot and we were all tired. It was late in the day. She said what she had to say, but it was in the middle of a paragraph and nobody heard her. I considered jumping up and making a loud noise and saying, "Did you hear what she just said?" But I didn't risk it. So the day came and went.

But that's true. The worst patriarchy for a woman is the interior one. I think the greatest threat to feminine consciousness is the patriarchal female.

JOHNSON: Which is a female overwhelmed by her male-ness, and our society is all geared for that. I had one for a mother. She was an extroverted sensation, Amazon, and that typology.

MCGEHEE: You wrote a book about femininity gained and lost, regained.

JOHNSON: I was young and foolish then.

VII.

WE AND THE TRISTAN/ISEULT MYTH

MCGEHEE: Why did you choose Tristan and Iseult for the myth for *We*?

JOHNSON: What else?

That's the myth for relationship for our time, and it's the only myth of all the great myths that ends disastrously. There is no solution to the Tristan and Iseult myth.

That doesn't bode very well for us. We need to complete it or finish it out, or I don't know what, but that myth says exactly what men and women are up against with each other now.

One detail of that myth, which took me some time to discover and more time to come to some terms with, is the fact that early on in the myth when Tristan and Iseult are spending time together and they have paid the price and they have established their right to be together and they have to break it up over and over. Lover's quarrels. It is so big, it is so high voltage, it is so powerful that they can't stand it, so they have to manage to break it up.

And people do that so frequently. Household will be going on pretty well. Somebody will throw a monkey wrench in the machinery. Human beings can't stand that high voltage. The thing one wants most of all, which could be solved or heard only in heaven, can't function on the face of the earth.

And the logical thing to do is to put it back in the church. But people don't seem to be able to do that.

MCGEHEE: You say put it back into the church?

JOHNSON: Yes. It's one's religious function. And there's all the mechanisms in the Church for receiving it, but it's not a language which seems tenable for modern people.

I watched in India. I mean old India, I avoided Westernized India, as bad as we are. And then watch the young people go to the temple and sit down cross-legged before the goddess and recite the mantras and do the ceremonies and go off into an ecstasy and get up and go home and treat their wife like an ordinary human being. Nobody expects his wife to go in the dark, so she didn't have to.

MCGEHEE: So through their ritual process, they're able to encounter the divine and don't expect that to be in their human relationship.

JOHNSON: That's right. And it works so well. Traditional Indian people with all their poverty and all the things that they have to bear. They're happy people.

We've got our levels crossed. It's as simple as that.

I'd like to write a book on levels, but it doesn't have a language for it.

India has 96 words for love. They have a vocabulary for differentiation. We don't.

How many men have come to my consulting room and starry look on their eyes? Well, I've fallen in love with my true love. I feel terrible and I'll never survive the guilt, but I have to leave my family. I try to talk levels to him, but his ears won't hear.

"*In* love" is the divine madness.

MCGEHEE: I have an analyst friend who says falling in love is the only psychosis not in the DSM-IV.

There's too much numinosity for the ego to handle, is that what you're saying?

JOHNSON: Needs a container and marriage is not an adequate container for it, though we try.

Somebody quite a while ago said the ego is soluble in three different things: love, madness, and alcohol. None of those are good containers. St. Theresa could say a thing or two about that.

MCGEHEE: The inner castle.

JOHNSON: Mhmm. I took a good friend of mine to the desert house. I have a house out in the desert and sometimes take people out to rest them up mostly. He's a scientist, PhD from a big university.

Put him to bed in his bedroom. One night I heard my bed shake, woke up, and here's this fellow. He said, Robert, I've been incinerated by love. He had.

He waivers around between understanding that it's a vision of God and some young woman that sets it off in him. He knows the difference. Often he's helpless between those two things. He's married, and got two kids.

MCGEHEE: We confuse the outer world marriage many times, as you would describe, in levels with the hieros gamos.

JOHNSON: That's right.

But somehow the church, whether it's its fault, our fault, or inevitably has lost its capacity to contain this high-voltage mystical vision. I don't know anybody anymore who goes to church and goes into an ecstatic trance at a vision of the ineffable. I don't know what to do practically about this.

VIII.

CHRISTIANITY AND WESTERN PSYCHE

MCGEHEE: Annie Dillard in her writing says, "We should take those signs from in front of the church that say 'Enter, Rest, and Pray,' and replace them with signs that say 'Enter at your own risk.'"

Did Jung say that religion came into being to protect us from God?

JOHNSON: Sounds like him.

Well, when religion got practical, it found out that it could sell the protection better than it could the conduction.

MCGEHEE: I know from your tradition you were raised Christian and have worked with many, many Christian clergy. You were at a Christian monastic, monastery at one time.

JOHNSON: Yes.

MCGEHEE: Do you consider yourself to be Christian still, Robert?

JOHNSON: Yes. In a profound way and it grows deeper and deeper and it grows more and more Catholic.

MCGEHEE: In this sense of universal?

JOHNSON: Well, my vocabulary gets thin at that point

MCGEHEE: You're not talking particularly about Roman Catholic

JOHNSON: No

MCGEHEE: Catholic in the sense of inclusivity, universality?

JOHNSON: Basic, say, but then the fundamentalists would say the same thing, and I'm not saying that. I don't know any aspect of Christian theology which has not proven to be highly effective and intelligible in practical life.

Jung also said that Christianity is the best roadmap of the Western psyche that exists. Poor Jung had so much difficulty with his Lutheran pastor father that he remained rebel for much of the time.

Joseph Campbell was in school when I was there. And he was an ardent Roman Catholic at the time. Much more outspoken than most people, certainly more than I.

The general atmosphere in the school was, "You're still going to church? Aren't you through your adolescence yet?"

He resented this. He'd come in in the morning and with that big resonant voice of his, he would say, "My, but Mass was fine this morning." People would shudder and look away.

It crashed for him later on and he got very angry with the church.

I have no quarrel with Christianity. I have lots of quarrel with how it's presented.

MCGEHEE: Would you say we're in a post-Christian era?

JOHNSON: Uh, let's say two things. Yes, we're in a post-Christian era, but as somebody else said, "maybe we will try out Christianity now for the first time." They're both true.

MCGEHEE: The archetypes of Christianity and the Christian myth still are viable. You feel for both, personally and for the collective?

JOHNSON: Yes. Certainly viable for the Western world. Now, whether for the East I don't know.

The Eastern archetypes don't work well or adequately for a Westerner. I learned that firsthand. It may be that the reverse is also true.

MCGEHEE: You felt that Krishnamurti tried to translate too many of the Eastern archetypes to the Western mind.

JOHNSON: Well, he didn't even do that. He wasn't a standardized guru coming from India and talking about the pantheon of India. He didn't do that. I think he himself was beyond that. But he didn't have anything to offer, a handhold on this vertical cliff. He wasn't a typical Indian teacher.

MCGEHEE: It still holds though for you, as Jung said, that it's very difficult for a Western man to become an Eastern man and vice versa.

JOHNSON: I think it's impossible.

I ran into lots of Westerners in India who were permanently affixed to an Ashram or Eastern. I never saw one that I thought was living a viable life.

They all clung to some sentimentality or some projection or some, some basically untenable life. And it won't have anything to do with the Eastern cults here in the West. That's not the point. We've got our own point, but we won't take it.

It's kind of fun to try with Eastern things because it's a new language and it's not so much tainted with my grandmother, my Baptist grandmother.

I doubt if Orthodox Christians would find me a Christian, but I think I am.

MCGEHEE: If Christianity is still a viable myth for Western culture, I've heard you say that literalism is idolatry. And that has in some ways trivialized our myth, has it not?

JOHNSON: By turning it into idolatry, it exteriorizes it and depotentiates it.

I was walking on the streets in Minneapolis one day. I'd gone there for lectures and I was walking home from Alan Whitman's Church, and minding my own business.

I can't say I've heard words from heaven, but that would be the best way I could describe it. I heard interiorly, but the only recourse I have is to talk about the words of it: "Now look, make up your mind, either everything is the body and blood of Christ or nothing is. Now make up your mind."

Well, I didn't fall flat, but I wasn't far from it. And I knew instantly on the spot if I come to the conclusion that nothing is the body and blood of Christ, I'm finished. There's no way to live. But to take everything as the body and blood of Christ, beyond me. Could be done only in a profoundly inner sense.

MCGEHEE: Back to levels again.

JOHNSON: Yes. I think if one went to Mass and heard and was touched by the drama which is being portrayed to one, one would be flattened out. Stagger out of the church, profoundly touched.

The church seems to have settled as a social or a fair or as a community matter, which is important. It teaches morality, not religion.

MCGEHEE: Religion is about experience.

JOHNSON: Religion, to take the word "apart" means to put things back together again.

"Ree-lig," L-I-G is the root of it, "ligature," to put back together again. That's the job of the religious life.

I think still in my life, if I found a good, honest monastery or ashram, I would go. I've given up trying.

I love to go to the Kamaldalese Monastery, which is just across the road from Esalen. They make a good pair of opposites.

JOHNSON: Good place to stop?

MCGEHEE: Etymologically speaking. It's from Ligare, which means to connect. Whatever's fractured, whatever's...

JOHNSON: To put together again. "Re" means again. And "lig" means to join together.

MCGEHEE: Psychologically speaking, the religious nature of psyche is that those things that are desperate, they come together. That's a religious function of psyche. The opposites, for instance.

JOHNSON: The Garden of Eden split us apart, and it's the job of the church to put us back together again. Simple as that.

MCGEHEE: So the religious function of psyche is about those things that are separate, being put together or integrated.

JOHNSON: Modern man is so driven by the brokenness or the opposites. You just watch people on the street and they're striving for something, I don't know, the brokenness.

I don't know why the church doesn't speak more powerfully than it does. It's partly because people don't want to hear the only thing that would help. It's not entirely the church's fault.

MCGEHEE: And what is it they don't want to hear?

JOHNSON: That there's something in the world greater than their ego.

MCGEHEE: The old traditions of sacrifice, surrender, detachment.

JOHNSON: I'm sick of the old stereotype 19th century Irish priest who gets up and harangues about suffering and sacrifice and so forth. That doesn't work either.

MCGEHEE: We're talking about it on another level.

JOHNSON: But where's the language for that?

MCGEHEE: It's in the sacred story, it's in the myth. But we hear it and we literalize it or concretize it.

JOHNSON: It is. But for an arrogant populace, me included, people don't want to hear it until they hurt so badly that they can't stand it.

If a suicide came to my consulting room, I would jump up and down and cheer and say, "Great, it's absolutely correct. It's the right thing to do. Just don't damage your body doing it."

MCGEHEE: Something needs to die.

JOHNSON: Mmhh....levels again.

MCGEHEE: Yeah.

IX.

THE GOLDEN WORLD

MCGEHEE: Robert, let's talk more about the golden world. You got that term from Mircea Eliade?

JOHNSON: That's right. We are venturing into a subject which is poverty-stricken in the English language. I don't know any terminology for such things as that. And somebody who is concerned with that or perhaps has an experience of it is utterly without language to cope with it.

My favorite illustration for this, the poverty-strickenness of Western, especially English language, is that Sanskrit has 96 words for love. Persian is 80, Greek is 3, and English is 1.

Well, what can you do with a subject like that? I don't dare tell somebody that I love you because of at least a dozen things am I saying. They generally take it at its worst. So that word is stricken out of my vocabulary, it's just not usable.

So when a new faculty is ready for differentiation—I'm talking about an individual now—it often turns up that one must make a differentiation that one didn't have before.

An example in my own life, "sensuous" and "sensual." I didn't know there was any difference between the two until my own development demanded a differentiation, and then I got to work. And those two words mean two different things, close but different.

"Sensual" means bestial or rough or rude or primitive. And "sensuous" means the spirit incarnated into matter. I need that differentiation, but most people don't know the difference when I'm talking about it.

So the golden world. I think it's what scripture speaks of as the kingdom of heaven.

We tend to literalize things and many things that are important in our Christian heritage are literalized, they're given an outer meaning, place, or time, or geography, which perhaps not the original intent.

I'm thinking that the kingdom of heaven is not some other time, other place. But, well, there my vocabulary fails me. It's a state of consciousness or it's an experience which is open to anyone, anytime, any place. I think the scriptural meaning of the Kingdom of Heaven is mostly lost to people because they literalize it.

An English poet, Owen Barfield, said that "literalism is idolatry." Well, I suddenly knew what idolatry was then, too. It means taking something and affixing it to the wrong level.

So, I have nicely evaded your question of the golden world.

MCGEHEE: One of the things I've liked about that scriptural reference is there are three different translations of Jesus' words.

Sometimes it's translated, "The kingdom of heaven is *among* you." Sometimes it's translated, "*In the midst* of you." Sometimes it is translated *within* you. And I'm satisfied that all three are true at once.

JOHNSON: Yes, and struggling to portray a mystery which is not easily defined. But if one is struck by the kingdom of heaven or the golden world, then one has to cope with it somehow.

MCGEHEE: I suspect when Jesus talked about "let those who have the ears hear and the eyes see," he was talking about the golden world.

JOHNSON: I think so.

MCGEHEE: What preparations are there for opening one's eyes and ears to the golden world? What disciplines or exercises are important?

JOHNSON: Well, I'll lapse into Hindu theology on that subject. The preparation for the kingdom heaven or the golden world or the beatific vision, that's another word for it.

In Hindu view, it consists chiefly of getting rid of the things that stand in the way of it. You can't get *it*. There's a phrase for such thought, the Nanak vision, finding out what *it* is not and what's left is *it*.

So one can scramble after a vision of heaven or the golden world. Almost everything that one does in the scramble department just obscures it even further. But if one can simplify, if one can get closer to the primal source or force, that's about all one can do to aid one's experience of the golden world. And more important than that is the question, can one stand it or how much can one stand it? It's not difficult to find enlightenment in the Eastern term for the golden world, but who can stand it? Can knock one completely off one's feet.

MCGEHEE: Like St. Paul.

JOHNSON: Yes. Knock you off your horse literally. And disastrously so, sometimes. The Psalms are full of people who got a glimpse of something bigger than they could stand.

MCGEHEE: I was asked in my propaedeuticum for my diploma as an analyst the difference between a religious experience and a psychotic event.

JOHNSON: One's capacity to stand it. Jung liked to point out that Nietzsche failed it. Nietzsche went psychotic and William Blake stood it.

What is the difference between a psychotic experience and a religious experience? It depends entirely on one's ability to stand or to handle the experience.

Such things happen frequently to people, much more frequently than our society likes to acknowledge. Some people sidestep it and evade the disaster of it, but lose its beauty too. Or some people go fanatical with it. Have to go out with their sandwich board on the street and proclaim the second coming of Christ, or some such thing.

But if one has the psychic strength to take it, it can be a religious experience of tremendous power.

Jung liked to point out that Nietzsche failed it, he identified with it.

Jung liked to point out the point in Nietzsche's poem, *Thus Speak Zarathustra*, where Jung thought that Nietzsche lost the battle.

At one point, Zarathustra comes to Nietzsche and insists that he take a frog and swallow it, the frog being earthy, goopy, uninspiring reality.

And Nietzsche tried, but he choked on it and spat it out. I forget what he said, but "none of that stuff for me." And Jung felt that Nietzsche lost the battle at that moment because he wouldn't take the earthiness of life.

He wouldn't take the, the just, stuff and boredom and mundane world.

Jung liked to point out that William Blake, having been offered much the same strength, the power of revelation, painted it and wrote it and related intelligently to it without identifying with it. And thus became a great artist.

Jung once said that William Blake went farther into the collective unconscious and lived to tell the tale than anybody else that he knew. Jung pointed out on the same subject that William Blake kept a very humble and ordinary and human life. He married and he earned his life as an engraver, earned his living as an engraver, and wouldn't live in London, lived in a little village. Jung said William Blake saved his sanity in that manner.

So the answer is, who can take it?

X.

OWNING YOUR OWN SHADOW

MCGEHEE: It's important if we're gonna talk about the golden world to talk about the dark realm, the shadowy, the primitive. I'm thinking as you were talking about Joseph Conrad having Kurtz going up the river and not being able to come back. Francis Ford Coppola popularized that story with Apocalypse Now.

JOHNSON: Yes. Well, language betrays us because the golden world is not all light. The true vision of the golden world contains as much darkness as it does light, but we have no terms for such a thing as that.

Long years ago, before World War II, Life magazine got some new color printing presses going. They had a wonderful exhibit of their ten-color printing. And they showed what each of the printing, apparently the paper goes through ten different presses to get the final gradations of color. And nine of them were the color. And he said, "now watch. There's no black yet." So the 10th one had added the black. And the 10th had a life and had a dimension to it that all the color ones, however complete they might be, didn't have. That's the best example I know of, the fact that an experience has to have its dark side or it has no completeness.

The golden world is an inadequate term.

MCGEHEE: I'm afraid that the phrase that you've coined for the collective "owning your own shadow" has been trivialized a bit by people assuming it's about, you know, I have this desire to lie or to cheat or to steal. It's much more substantial than that, isn't it Robert, in terms of the chaos of the psyche and the unconscious?

JOHNSON: Yeah. I've heard people who ought to know better talk about, "well, one of my shadow characteristics is." Well, by definition, a shadow is a part of you don't know. You don't talk about your own shadow. If you can talk about it, it's already conscious and it's no longer a shadow. Maybe just a bad habit now.

von Franz once said, "People occasionally say, 'Tell me what you think my shadow is.'" She said she'll never bite on that one. First of all, he wouldn't believe it, and second, he'd be angry.

These revelations must come in some kind of coherent order so that one can take it. Some aspect of the unconscious way down deep is constellated, which can happen. It will set on fire all of the layers of the unconscious anterior to rather above it. And you have a major explosion on your hands. Best to un-peel it layer by layer if one's lucky enough to do it that way.

MCGEHEE: In a safe container or context.

JOHNSON: Yes.

MCGEHEE: That's what analysis is about after all, isn't it?

JOHNSON: Yeah.

MCGEHEE: Providing a "temenos" or sacred circle or container.

JOHNSON: Yes, yes. One needs all the help one can get with such an experience.

MCGEHEE: That's why in the great spiritual traditions a guide or a leader, teacher, guru is important.

JOHNSON: Uh-huh.

MCGEHEE: But it's been abused, has it not?

JOHNSON: Yes, it's true that the guide or the Savior has been badly misunderstood or misused.

Mankind is such a bunch of evaders that they've turned Christianity into, "Well, I don't have to do this because Jesus died for my sins and that's adequate." Well he may have paved the way for understanding it, but one has to go one's own way with it.

I have another quarrel similar to this, the way analytical work is set up nowadays using the medical model. People come to the analyst and they unconsciously presume, "Well, I've done my part. I gave you a check. Now heal me." It doesn't work that way.

I consider an analyst as a guide in the sense that he carries some tools and he's trodden this path before, but he keeps two steps in back of his patient.

MCGEHEE: There are two sayings about that that occur to me, Jung saying that you can only take the student as far as he himself was gone. And then the Sufi saying that when the student's ready, the teacher appears.

JOHNSON: Yes.

The stories about Jung…a famous scientist came to him, laid out his problems. He says, "All right, what shall we do?" Jung says, "I haven't the foggiest idea. Let's look at your dreams." Dreams are a wonderful guide. They're a road map.

MCGEHEE: You say a lot about dream work in your book *Inner Work*.

JOHNSON: Yes.

MCGEHEE: Could you say something about the individual's work with his or her own dreams?

JOHNSON: I've racked my brains to try and get a simple, workable definition of a dream. The dream is information you should have, but don't. That says it, pretty clearly. It's information you should have.

There are no superfluous dreams. And one can never presume that you already know what the dream is talking about or the dream wouldn't bother you with it.

MCGEHEE: I've heard you say that you shudder when you hear the word dream interpretation.

JOHNSON: Well, yes. I have no truck with the books which elucidate dream symbols. This means this and that means that. Well, maybe it does and maybe it doesn't.

If one can use a dream book as a set of possibilities to get you started, that's useful. But it's no dictionary.

MCGEHEE: You've said only the dreamer can interpret his dream.

JOHNSON: That's right. He needs some help with it.

One has a huge resistance against one's dream. An analyst spends so much of his time, tactfully asking or suggesting or encouraging or challenging or maybe offering a possibility, but not more than that.

MCGEHEE: Jung said that the myth is to the collective as the dream is to the individual. How do you see that?

JOHNSON: I think that's well put. One is dreaming one's own mythology, and it's extremely important to know one's myth.

One's psychological myth, what else could it be, is as unique to one as one's own genetic structure is. The latter is accepted as scientific fact. One's DNA is unique, as one's fingerprint or the iris of one's eye. One's myth is as unique and it's as important to know who one is and that can best be described in mythological terms.

MCGEHEE: The dream maker seems to be concerned about wholeness and individuation. My training as an analyst was on the theoretical model that dreams compensate.

What is the compensatory function of dreams as you understand it?

JOHNSON: I agree, most dreams are compensatory, but they're not confined to that.

A dream would be compensatory if one is doing too much of something, or too little of something, and the dream will come along in its inimitable way, point out that you've been too loud, or you've been too shy, or you've been too something or another. The dream is compensatory in that sense.

And if the dream wants to point something out, it will often exaggerate it. That's compensatory too.

One can even say that an exaggeration in a dream is a degree of exaggeration of that which the dream is compensating. Yes, some utterly idiotic personality turns up in a dream, it's compensating an equally idiotic show-offness in one's daily personality.

Dreams often will bring up a new content, something not yet known to one. Big dreams are often of this nature. They will point out the next piece of road map which you're to be concerned with. I don't think that can be viewed as compensatory.

XI.

THE ORDERED UNIVERSE

MCGEHEE: Compensation is a big part of, I think, universal energy. Jung was quite taken with Heraclitus term enantiodromia, which means "running counter to," which is basically the theory of opposites. You've spoken before about inflation and deflation. These are the rules of the universe, as it were.

JOHNSON: Absolutely. Physics works on this principle. Virtually everything that happens is the interplay of the pair of opposites, positive and negative electricity or distribution of energy, whatever it might be. That's just as direct and applicable in psychology.

If you're going to ask me about the 9/11 event, we will have to view it in such terms as that.

MCGEHEE: Let's talk about the terrorist attack on this country and how you see it from a psychodynamic.

JOHNSON: Yes. I try to talk this out with people and I get virtually nowhere with it. The best response I get out of most people is a polite change of subject.

I've worked hard at this. I've come to a several-step way of approaching it. One must confirm each of the steps before one could hazard the next one.

The first one is that I believe in an ordered universe. A nice polite way of saying I believe in God, but that's not very good terminology anymore. I believe in an ordered universe that things happen for an intelligent reason, possibly beyond my intelligence, but nonetheless intelligent.

Second, that reality consists of pairs of opposites. I can retreat to physicists for confirmation of this. Everything that happens in the physical world is an interplay of opposites. Positive electricity reacts with negative and charged electricity.

I think it's humorous that they got them wrong from the beginning. negative charge goes toward the positive, but they didn't get around to changing the name. And everything, everything, every happening is an interplay of opposites, masculine, feminine, acid, alkaline, on and on.

If you're still with us on these issues, then one can hazard or surmise a third point. And that is that if one of a pair of opposites gets out of hand or gets too large or is more highly charged than the polarity of that pair of opposites can stand, something takes place to rectify that imbalance.

So if you're still with me, one can ask a horrendous question: what imbalance required 9/11?

That's a hard one. One can't blame somebody else. There are a lot of things one can't do. But if one has the humility to ask that question, what imbalance required the events in New York City? I think one can get somewhere.

One could speak very simply about it. Best way, something went too tall and needed to come down. Well, the ramifications of that, something got too rich and needed to be leveled. The high places shall be brought down, the low places exalted. I think the big events of the world are of that nature.

I have to hang on hard to hold onto my original statement that everything has meaning because sometimes I can't hang on that far, but I believe it. One could talk for a long time about what went too far in one direction and constellated its opposite.

There's Jung's words that he used so often, the "enantiodromia," something turning into its opposite or precipitating its opposite.

Modern people don't like to think this way, though. We're much more likely to figure out who was the villain and who's doing it wrong and how can we get him to think like we think. That doesn't go anywhere.

Small example of this, just a personal example. I'm not very good at riding bicycles, but I got a bicycle in India. Managed pretty well. I was leaving a friend's house at night and just got the first second of momentum on the bicycle, turned to waive goodbye to my friend, lost my balance and fell in the sewer. Sewers are just the gutters in the street in India. I thought, "Okay, that'll teach me a lesson."

One's lucky if just falling into the sewer is enough to wake one up.

MCGEHEE: Could you venture to say any more about what you think the inflation of the Twin Towers, and the fall, would imply for our culture and our collective psyche is?

JOHNSON: Well, there's too much "up" in our society. Up in a very general sense of too fast, too much excess of anything. If one has what one has, it seems never to be enough and the American mentality needs more.

And I'm privately of the opinion that the basic direction of consciousness changed just within living memory. And "up" has been the way to heaven for as long as written language has been around. It's simply built into our language, built into our structure. Good things are up. I'm feeling up this morning. Yeah, I'm on my way up to success or climbing the ladder or the ascent of Mount Carmel. These things are so basically built into our language.

I think when language was being constructed, and when our scriptures were being put together, the world was so down and people were living in such close proximity to the mud that they had to be told about the up. People were scrambling so hard for just the physical stuff of life that they had to be reminded that there's a spirit.

But suddenly, historically speaking, we got up. The last two centuries have crossed the median line and we're too fast and we're too up and we're too ambitious and we're too busy and we're too rich and we're too fat and we're too all kinds of things on the side which was deficit before.

So if one watches contemporary dreams, down is good now. That is for a member of our up society. The value lies in a downward movement. And we don't hear that. The church hasn't heard it. But I think fate is trying to inform us that we're too high, too fast, too much, too rich, too fat, too excessive in our expectations or demands.

And we're getting battered from all sides, not hearing yet. How many more, whatever it takes to humble us down to the midpoint. Not back to the mud again, but to an even point.

MCGEHEE: Once again about balance.

JOHNSON: Balance. And you cannot cope with balance without a basic understanding or acknowledgement of pairs of opposites. I can't cope with anything anymore without going back to the very beginning of experience or existence of what pair of opposites is involved and what mismanagement or imbalance has occurred. People don't know how to think that way though.

MCGEHEE: Robert, Jung said all "isms" are negative. How do you understand material*ism*? Why is this such a culture of material*ism*?

JOHNSON: There's nothing wrong with material. But putting "ism" on the end of it, turns it into blasphemy. Material is perfectly good. God saw fit to incarnate into the material world. Very basic statements of Christianity take material into consideration.

But I think the church was speaking to the condition of its time where material was eating everything up. And just to get the next mouthful of food or save yourself from your neighbor was the paramount stuff of life. And it turned into material*ism* and quickly became spiritual*ism*, which is just as bad an ism as materialism.

And we have suffered an enantiodromia now, just within living memory. Old people remember when such a basically different attitude prevailed. I remember people talking about Midwest childhood. We never locked the door. Never thought of such a thing. Now, it takes about four keys to get into this building.
(laughs)

So this pendulum swing of opposite turning into opposites. I told you about my perpetual deflation early in my life. Fritz Kunkel opened up worlds for me. And the pendulums swung violently into positive inflation. It went around like a jackass, showing off. Fate was kind enough to knock me down off that.

Now that's the first thing to ask when one is pursuing some psychological or interior issue, what pair of opposites are at work?

Active imagination is a wonderful tool for setting up a dialogue between pairs of opposites or among pairs. You personify both of the pairs of opposites and get them to dialogue in and see what they can teach each other. It's never a matter of one is right and the other is wrong. The farther one goes into the unconscious, the more inadequate right and wrong becomes. It's imbalance, how much?

MCGEHEE: I love what you say about guilt means you've taken sides.

JOHNSON: (laughs) Yes. I used to tease my Baptist grandmother and tell her that guilt was a sin. Oh she'd get furious because it was her chief comfort. If she wasn't wringing her hands, she wasn't happy. I still got my grandmother inside me too.

XII.

THE SELF AND GOD

MCGEHEE: I don't know when we will understand the simple admonition that certain things that we get from our myths or from our sacred stories or our fairy tales that when turned to the outer world its superstition when turned to the inner world its wisdom.

JOHNSON: That's well put.

Do I believe in the virgin birth of Christ? Outwardly, it's foolish. Superstition.

Inwardly, it's the only possible explanation for the birth of the redemptive figure within one's own psyche. It has to be a virgin birth. That means of one parent, that means it's a totally introverted process, and it's not the interaction of two things in the usual sense of the word.

So the whole subject of incest, which is taboo to the point where one can scarcely discuss it even, is touching upon that experience which does not come from opposites. And our language can't cope with that. But when somebody dreams it, they have to cope with it.

MCGEHEE: Jung said incest as an archetype is about wholeness, but acted out in the outer world is horrifying.

JOHNSON: Yes.

MCGEHEE: What's that Sufi saying you like so much? I saw myself. I loved myself.

JOHNSON: I don't know the Sufi one, but there's an alchemical saying: "I mated with myself. I impregnated myself. I gestated myself. I gave birth to myself. I am myself."

MCGEHEE: That's the one. That's the ultimate incest, isn't it?

JOHNSON: And there's no understanding that, with ordinary modern mentality. Well, the psychological equivalent of incest is introversion. If you want to generate a new center of gravity for yourself, go off and be quiet. It's that kind of generation which will create the self in Jungian language.

MCGEHEE: Let's talk about the self. That paradoxical term is so difficult for consciousness to get a mind around. Jung said at one time that it's essence and it speaks another time as it is totality. So we moderns don't think paradoxically, do we Robert?

JOHNSON: We just act it. Paradox unexamined as neurosis, paradox taken consciously is revelation.

One is wandering beyond human concept when he tries to talk about the self in the Jungian sense. The best he could do was to talk about self, small "s," "I" or "self," capital "S," the big sense. But if you experience it, and back to our original conversation, you have to make it conscious or go mad.

Then one's got to have some conscious relationship to the self. I wish so much I could go to the church and get down on my knees and put my forehead on the floor and honor the self, the icon at the altar. I can't do it that way. I tried so hard.

I'll tell you the moment that the Church died in an exterior sense for me. The Church has not died in an interior sense, thank God. But I decided that some great people in history had gotten great solace from the Virgin Mary. So OK, I'm going to have a try again. I chose a

Catholic church in Los Angeles endowed by a wealthy oil family. They had done a wonderful reproduction of the Spanish Baroque church on Adams Avenue in Los Angeles. Beautiful building. Sculptures are superb. Not the plastered kind of thing that makes you shudder, but superb things. I hung around and waited until there was nobody else in the church, a Tuesday afternoon or something. So with my knees shaking, I went over to the statue of the Virgin and knelt down and began pouring my heart out to her. I focused and found out that her halo was a neon light. That did it. I got up and left, never came back.

I might do better now. I don't know. Neon light's okay.

MCGEHEE: The self.

JOHNSON: The self. Especially the feminine self, or the feminine aspect of the self.

Parvati on my table here, the lamp, the oil lamp, is a symbol of that. She's the goddess of compassion. She stands on a table there holding a bowl of oil with a small lip and a wick. Light the lamp of compassion. When I got Parvati in India, I asked, "What kind of oil do I use?" "Coconut oil." "Oh, why coconut oil?" "Cheapest." I use olive oil here.

MCGEHEE: Jung took the idea from the Hebrew scriptures of the Imago Dei, the image of God, and posited that the self, which is simply a word that points to a mystery, but the self is the image of God within each of us. And then he loved this idea from Rudolf Otto in the book called *The Idea of the Holy*, of the numinous or the numinous energy of the Imago Dei or self within.

JOHNSON: Yes. I love obscure words, trying to describe the mystery because I can't pull them out of the mystery. Numinous, or the tremendum, the mystery. God cannot be portrayed for a Jew, not even the word.

India portrayed God as zero, is the unsayable. And mathematicians got hold of it and made use of it and changed the whole system of mathematics in the world. All they had before was the Roman numerals, which can't do very much with.

I can't imagine living without a concept of zero mathematically. I cannot conceive of what it would be like not to know what a zero is, but it set the whole of modern mathematics into motion. Can't cope with mathematics without a zero. And somebody made the joke that India invented the zero, which is true, and fell in love with it. That's their problem now. They literalized it.

One can talk around the mystery, talk around God. But that doesn't seem very rewarding to me.

MCGEHEE: Meaning what?

JOHNSON: What do you mean?

MCGEHEE: It's not rewarding to you to talk around God.

JOHNSON: That's right. I get no closer to the mystery.

MCGEHEE: I see. So much of Western theology is logos or logic or talking about God rather than experiencing God.

JOHNSON: Yes. That word "about" is eloquent. I get tired of it. The worst is happening to me, I'm getting tired of words. All words are inexact.

MCGEHEE: For a man who's sold over two million copies with words.

JOHNSON: I know. It's ridiculous. I make my money with words and don't like them.

MCGEHEE: What about the dream with your pen ink turning to water?

JOHNSON: Yes. Five, six, seven, eight, nine, ten years ago, I had a simple dream. I was writing with my pen, but instead of ink, it had water. I should have quit then.

MCGEHEE: One of the things Jung said about the self is that we project the self, and that certain historical figures have constellated those projections. So he says that the Christ is a symbol of self, the Atman for the Hindus, the Buddha for the Buddhists.

What's your experience with that as misunderstood and literalized and concretized? And the idea of sentimentality about those figures, which is just an instrument's opposites, which would be brutality.

JOHNSON: That's a very difficult one.

Ordinary mortals can't stand to look upon the living God. Moses had to go hide his head while God walked by. So we need places or people or circumstances to project that which is too great for a human to bear.

There's a custom in India, which thank God I knew about before I got there. One has the right to go to somebody, anybody, a stranger, somebody on the street, man or woman, old or young, and ask that person if he or she will be the incarnation of God for you. Well, what a custom.

I got into deeper water than I could cope with. The only time India got me down, I was in Calcutta and I was alone. I just couldn't take it anymore. The awfulness of India. Calcutta, I think, must be the bottom of the world. I couldn't stand it.

So I remembered that one could ask help from somebody. There was the appropriate language to use. So in desperation I went out to hunt for the incarnation of God for me, something to hang on to. I went out to a park nearby, feeling better already. I looked at various people coming and going, and who was going to catch it from me. Finally, I chose a middle-aged Indian, nothing to distinguish him from ten million other people, Indian clothing. But he walked with grace and dignity.

So I went up to him, asked him if he spoke English. He said, "Yes." That was a good start. The second sentence to that man was, "Will you be the incarnation of God for me?" And he looked at me very seriously. And he said, "Yes."

So I poured out my woes. I scarcely stopped to breathe between sentences and told him who I was and what had happened. I was at the end of my rope and I couldn't stand it and I needed help. And I was ten thousand miles from home and about to explode with all the things that were happening, on and on, on and on.

Okay, I wound down. Felt better. So I thanked him. He hadn't said a word. Bowed, and I said, "Then who are you?" Got my manners back. The man absolutely knocked me over backward, He said, "I'm a Roman Catholic priest." Which is not common in India. And how I had chosen a Roman Catholic priest to be the incarnation of God for me, I don't know, but it worked. Completely dumbfounded, He bowed, I bowed, and we walked off. I'll never forget him, and I doubt if he'll ever forget me.

So it's true, one must put the Imago Dei somewhere. No mortal is capable of standing that kind of numinosity. But pity the poor man that people put the image of God upon. No way can they personally hold it.

The Roman Church is in a big turmoil now because some of their priests who are the incarnation of God on the face of the earth for them have been caught misbehaving. This is a big disillusionment.

But music or poetry, one's imaginative life. Some of our festivals and ceremonies still carry those things. Hollywood would like to usurp it, but they don't do a very good job. Can't say anymore.

MCGEHEE: It's interesting to me that as we look at the incarnation of God that many times we only look to sacred spaces or sacred places or sacred people but Mircea Eliade and his *Sacred and Profane* says many times the sacred's camouflaged in the profane.

JOHNSON: Do you know the origin of those two words sacred and profane?

MCGEHEE: Help me.

JOHNSON: "Sacred" was the ceremony that went on for the elite or the aristocrats *inside* the church. And the word "profane" means the porch of the church. And the morality plays were played out on the porch of the church, but it was the same thing as had been going on inside. So the sacred and the profane are just, are the same thing, focused at different levels.

MCGEHEE: You said recently at a conference in Kanuga that you were coming home, lecturing no more, writing no more, and to work on the golden world. What does that look like, Robert?

JOHNSON: How could I tell you?

It consists mostly of saving my energy, having more time for introversion, and reducing down the things that get in the way of the golden world, because it, the golden world, is there all the time. It's a big misconception to think that you produce it or even earn it.

Sorry, I can't say any more.

MCGEHEE: No more need be said.

XIII.

LOVE

MCGEHEE: You indicated previously that one of the great problems of our time is the problem of love, the problem of romantic love, authentic love, the paltry, western understanding of love. And of course you've written about it extensively in your book *We* based on the Tristan and Isolde myth. But let's talk for a moment about how this got perverted in the western world and what's our way out of that.

JOHNSON: And it's true, it's a problem in the western world, though it's spreading all over the world now. Old India has nothing to do with romantic love. They don't know what it is. Go back to attitudes and the words in back of attitudes now. We have to have two kinds, at least two words for love, because there are at least two kinds, if not ninety-six kinds, of love. One is ordinary love.

Friend of mine with genius calls it "stir the oatmeal," the kind of love serving, ordinary, keep the kitchen, work, the everyday-ness of relatedness. And there's not much fireworks in that kind of love. It's a humble, mundane, livable, and sustainable love.

Then there's romantic love, which is a hundred thousand volt streak of fire which falls upon one and when it's often awakened by another person, that's the *in* love. We have that much differentiation. We talk about love and we talk about the *in* love. We've gone that far with it.

And they're both real, tremendously real. The *in* love or the romantic love or the hundred thousand volt visitation from heaven is generally the biggest religious experience that ordinary man ever has. And he's miserably ill-equipped to cope with it. It happens to most people. As I said, it's often the one experience of the tremendum or the self or the vision of God which one is likely to have in a lifetime.

But we Westerners and not Easterners, they know better. But we almost automatically ask a fulfillment of this romantic love from another human being. And it just happens that human beings can't produce 100,000 volt replies. Though they try. So we make the mistake of basing their marriages on the romantic love model. Scarcely knowing, not knowing that no human being, oneself or one's partner, can bear up under this. It's something outside of time and space. It's something outside a human can...

If one has the courage to go back and read one's love letters, they're full of things "forever" and "I will die for you" and permanent and big, big, big things, 100 volts, 100,000 volt size.

Well, ordinary relationship can't bear up under this. It just can't. It's just not built for it. Babies and diapers and mortgages and dull mornings and things like that, can't hold up under that expectation.

The word "honeymoon" means that it'll be sweet for a month. One goes off to live in heaven for a month, and if one makes a transition and come back, well, one can make a human-sized marriage out of what one has. But most people go away with a terrible sense that they got cheated, or they got misrepresented, or they didn't get what they hoped for, or something went wrong. Well nothing went wrong except the placement of this tremendous 100,000 volt religious experience. One gets almost nowhere trying to talk with a modern person about this.

I remember a teenage boy looking at me, with anguish on his face, and he said, "Are you telling me I shouldn't fall in love?" I said, Well, you couldn't stop it if you tried, and it's too valuable. But I can get you to think about where it is appropriate, and you don't have to be disillusioned because fair maiden, who received the full brunt of this lightning bolt from heaven, doesn't live up to everything you thought she would be.

And I'm asked what to do about this, and practically speaking, I don't know. We insist on the mythological, "Fall in love and marry and live happily ever after" myth, and it doesn't work that way.

Love, which is the awareness of another human being, as she or he actually is, human size, is durable and it's livable and it doesn't have a lot of fireworks with it, but that's the stuff of marriage.

Now, what to do with the fireworks and the hundred thousand volts that stands absolutely unanswered in our culture.

I watch young Hindu men go to the temple and They sit cross-legged before the image of the goddess and do their yoga and do their prayers and drift off into an ecstasy. Often they're shaking, they're trembling. And they wake up and get up and go off to work and go home and treat their wives as human beings Which seems very lowkey, it seems uneventful. That's a lot saner than what we're doing. But I don't know what to do.

MCGEHEE: How did the idea, the sentimentalized idea of romantic love, get into the Western mind?

JOHNSON: It's fairly recent. Only from approximately 16th century did it get common in our culture. There are examples in the works of art prior to that, but they were the extraordinary people.

The Catharist heresy that was banished as a heresy about 12th century came in from India. And it was like an epidemic that got going. I think maybe Western man was evolved just enough so that he was subject to something like that.

MCGEHEE: The Cathars.

JOHNSON: Yes.

And going in the aristocrats of Europe as troubadours, minnesingers, goddess singers, and various other odd kinds of courting fair maiden, but never touching her.

The Troubadour has to sing to an already married woman and win heart and get a handkerchief or a rosebud from her and go away and never see her again. Well, that's not very popular these days.

The Pope, I've forgotten which one, and I've forgotten the exact dates, decided that this was heretical and not consistent with Christianity. So he announced that this was a heresy. And since the root of it was in a small town in southern France called Albi, it's known as the Albigensian heresy. And supposedly that was the last ever heard of it. But that's not true because it went underground and turns up as romanticism now.

I think it was a mistake to count it a heresy because it went underground and became a pathology. I don't know what to do with it. I have a vivid history of that in my own life, but I wouldn't dare tell you about it.

MCGEHEE: How tempting.

JOHNSON: Well, I can go as far as to tell you that it became the root of my religious life, because that's what it's for.

Dr. Jung says that the anima, that's the feminine side of a man, and that's what jumps with a hundred thousand volts when you fall in love, is correctly viewed as the intermediary between the person and the deep parts of the unconscious. We make the mistake of thinking that she is the intermediary between oneself and somebody out there.

Well, I beat myself bloody raw on that one. Lived to tell the tale. And I found a way of—I dislike the word "use"—living that quality in a religious dimension.

And I won't tell you more.

MCGEHEE: When we project our anima onto a living female human being, we're often running to an inflation…

JOHNSON: It's a madness.

MCGEHEE: To a religious experience, to an infatuation, and intoxication. We tend not to make good choices or decisions in that state of altered consciousness.

JOHNSON: One's not looking at the girl that one's concerned with, one's looking at a divine image when it's put upon her. Maybe she'll play that out for you for a time.

MCGEHEE: When the projection collapses.

JOHNSON: Then there's bitterness. Marriages are falling apart now because they don't hold on the old glue, so to speak.

Free love is not the answer. I don't know what answer there is.

MCGEHEE: The institution of marriage for most of the history of humankind has been the arranged marriage.

JOHNSON: Yeah. A contract. That's what it is in India. You can't talk that to an American.

MCGEHEE: Love emanated out of the relationship rather than initiating the relationship. Is that correct?

JOHNSON: Tell me again?

MCGEHEE: Then the arranged marriage, the contract was that we would make domestic partnership and love, whatever we mean by that, would emanate out of the relationship rather than love initiating the relationship.

JOHNSON: Well, that's the poverty of our vocabulary. Because the arranged marriage is a form of love and they have a word for it.

The thing is that we don't have any other place to put the numinous experience of romanticism.

We ask another person to be our salvation or the center of our life or the meaning of everything. Nobody can do that, either way. Most marriages turn into a kind of make the best of something that didn't work very well.

MCGEHEE: Does it help to walk around a bit in the Greek words "eros," "philia," or "agape?" Maybe we could get a little more help, a larger consciousness about this divine gift of love that we're so paltry in our consciousness about?

JOHNSON: Yes.

MCGEHEE: Eros, Philia, Agape.

JOHNSON: Yeah. Even that's too limited.

MCGEHEE: What does Eros mean for us today, Robert?

JOHNSON: Usually it means a sexual attraction. Genital love, which is love. But when you have only one or two or three possible concepts of love, love your neighbor, they tend to get exclusive or doesn't hold up well.

Imagine having 96 words for love. It'd have the exact word to bring forth: love of your friend, love of your wife, love of your mistress, love of your priest, love of your horse or the sunset. But I don't know Sanskrit. It wouldn't help me much if I did.

I make a joke, Sanskrit has 96 words for love and one word for bolts and nuts. We have 96 words for bolts and nuts and one word for love. They're foundering on the bolts and nuts side of life, and we're foundering on the, what we're going to call our inadequacy of love.

MCGEHEE: Philia is the brotherly, sisterly love. We know of that as rich religious tradition and psychological mental hygiene to have Philia in your life.

JOHNSON: There's so many others.

We're breaking our teeth on the homosexual quality now. India takes that in a stride.

MCGEHEE: Why do you think there's so much homophobia in our culture?

JOHNSON: Well, we've evolved to a point where we have to differentiate and we're dragging our feet. People, cultures drag their feet terribly when something new turns up.

A Hindu boy is married to his buddy at ten. I'm shocked to use the word "married," but there's a ceremony. It's a blood exchange.

That's what blood brother means, not genetically from the same family, it means that they exchange blood. And that's for life. And at 16, he's married to his wife, and those three people make a unit for the rest of their lives.

And a boy will spend more time with his buddy than he will with his wife. If he goes on vacation, he doesn't go with his wife, he goes with his buddy.

And she's got a buddy—stretching language all over the place now—and is remarkably well satisfied with that arrangement. Husband and wife don't expect so much out of each other.

As Jack Sanford says, "So many marriages collapse under the excessive expectations of marriage."

I have a scholarship for Temagami, the summer conference of Journey into Wholeness. I've offered it to two of my friends. First to one. Oh, he wants to go.

He came back next day. "No, my wife won't let me go." Offered it to another friend, "Oh, yes." Next day, "sorry, I can't do it. My wife would be furious."

That kind of possessiveness, which, people, people just can't hold it.

MCGEHEE: The dark side of Eros says it now, the possessiveness.

JOHNSON: Well, that's overpowering the word "eros" too. I don't know how to talk about this with no vocabulary. Can't go to the hardware shop with just one word for bolts and nuts.

MCGEHEE: Well, let's just explore Agape for a minute so we'd be responsible to the Greeks.

JOHNSON: Hardly anybody knows what it means.

I know people who say that language forms consciousness. I don't know, I tend to argue that. But if it's true, our poverty of language indicates a poverty of capacity for consciousness.

We can't just invent a new word unless we make a new path of consciousness that would correspond with it or vice versa.

If a 50-year-old comes to my consulting room and he's fallen in love with his secretary, and is absolutely just gone, just beyond control or discipline, but he doesn't want to chuck his wife and children and tear up her marriage. So he sits there mutely looking at me. I try to teach him how to worship the new love, but don't try and make a sexual or marriage arrangement out of it.

Generally you can't comprehend this. That's what a Hindu does. Not in the form of another human being, certainly not in his immediate environment.

But the hundred thousand volt love is of the nature of worship, it's not of the nature of human relationship.

MCGEHEE: Hollywood's no help.

JOHNSON: Terrible detriment. Much of this is turning into bitterness in people now. Disillusionment. It's a wonderful word if one can stand it. But in its usual sense, it just means one gives up.

MCGEHEE: Well, the opposite of idealism is cynicism. And we find a cynical voice about love in our culture too.

JOHNSON: It's stuff for the cartoonist now.

MCGEHEE: Agape, by tradition, is God's love or the love of God or the love that God has for us. Which is the love that lets be or the love that empowers or the love that...

JOHNSON: Yeah. What does that mean to most people? Not much.

One can talk for twenty minutes to somebody in the romantic dilemma. He listens politely and after a while he says, "Okay, now what do I do?"

I tell him it's not a matter of doing, it's being. If you can stand that, we'll go on. If not, we haven't got much to talk about.

The worst problem.

XIV.

THE EVOLVING CONSCIOUSNESS

MCGEHEE: It seems to me that the idea of metanoia, of all the "noias," it's my favorite. Paranoia is being outside your mind. Metanoia is to change your mind. I think we have to change our mind, change our attitude, consciousness, consciousness, consciousness.

JOHNSON: To be beyond mind, "meta." That doesn't sell well.

MCGEHEE: No.

JOHNSON: I don't know what does sell now. Pharmacy sells. Pharmacopeia sells now. You can numb it out.

The number of people who take tranquilizers in this culture is frightening.

I heard somebody the other day say, the first time I had heard it and it socked me. "Well, I go home, turn on the TV and numb out."

I understand. It hurts too much to stand 24 hours a day.

MCGEHEE: It's almost as though it appears that consciousness is unnatural. Because we do it, it's so, with such difficulty.

JOHNSON: I think consciousness is a part of nature, but that's not a common idea.

MCGEHEE: Consciousness is evolving, is it not? I mean, in the individual, of course, we see it in the infants who are struggling to become conscious. But are we evolving consciously as a collective Robert?

JOHNSON: Not as a body. We're trying out other things. We're trying out science, which is a misuse of the word again.

It's my own quiet private opinion that we're going to have to have a big suffering before we will look deeper.

MCGEHEE: Part of the opportunity of the 9/11 is for changed consciousness.

JOHNSON: Yes. And just look what, what and who picked that up and took it off in another direction. Another war.

Hard to keep from being a pessimist.

Well, I know what to do with an individual, but I haven't any idea what our culture should or could do.

MCGEHEE: Jung felt that our future hung on the individual.

JOHNSON: It does. I'm sure of that.

There are old legends that there's a hermetic circle, a few conscious people, and that's what will keep civilization pulled together.

MCGEHEE: Those who commit to consciousness.

JOHNSON: Not just the ones who talk about it around the bookshops.

MCGEHEE: Talking about the people who are willing to suffer the consciousness.

JOHNSON: Yes. And the word "suffer" originally meant to allow. Not to wring your hands and drip blood.

MCGEHEE: I always love that King James version of the Sermon on the Mount where he says "Suffer the little children." It means really to allow them to come forward, to carry them up. To suffer something means to carry it, doesn't it?

JOHNSON: What did that turn up in more recent translations?

MCGEHEE: To um, permit.

JOHNSON: Oh, okay.

MCGEHEE: Teilhard de Chardin talks about the Omega Point, toward which all creation is moving.

JOHNSON: Yes. Creation thinks in terms of hundreds of thousands of years. I can't wait.

MCGEHEE: There must be an individual as well as a collective omega form.

JOHNSON: True. That's part of one's mythology.

My grandmother had it all taped in sweet, sweet and happy days in the goodbye and bye.

MCGEHEE: Are you optimistic about the next realm?

JOHNSON: What realm?

MCGEHEE: We're in it, aren't we?

JOHNSON: No, I'm not optimistic about it. Eventually, of course.

I have a new friend, a Roman Catholic priest, a young man. He comes down and we talk about things. I haven't talked about this have I?

MCGEHEE: No.

JOHNSON: Okay. It's remarkably free and open, but I'm wary of landing in with more than the poor man could stand.

One day I said, "Father, there was a heresy that I liked so much, but I've forgotten the name of it. It's the idea that there's no ultimate or permanent hell. Everybody makes his way to salvation, to heaven.

"Oh," he said, "yeah, that's the universalist heresy. Pope so and so on such and such a date branded that as a heresy."

So I thought maybe I could risk a little bit more, and I said, "You know, I believe this."

And he said, "Don't ever quote me, but I do too."

Yeah, it'll all work out.

There's a Chinese proverb: If you're invaded, if your country is invaded, welcome them. You'll assimilate them in three generations.

Enough, Father?

MCGEHEE: Thank you, Robert.

JOHNSON: Okay.

J. Pittman McGehee, Sr., D.D. is an Episcopal priest and Jungian analyst in private practice in Austin, Texas and is trustee emeritus of The Jung Center in Houston, Texas. He is widely known as a lecturer and educator in the field of analytical psychology and religion, as well as a published poet and essayist. He is the author of *The Invisible Church: Finding Spirituality Where You Are* (Praeger Press, 2008), *Raising Lazarus: The Science of Healing the Soul* (2009), *Words Made Flesh, The Paradox of Love and Growing Down* (selected poems) now available for sale through The Jung Center of Houston's Bookstore, Amazon.com and other fine booksellers.

J. Pittman McGehee, Jr., Ph.D. is a licensed psychologist in private practice in Austin, Texas. He received his doctorate from The University of Texas, Austin, focusing his research on the connection between psychological health and the concepts of mindfulness and self-compassion. In addition to his private practice, Dr. McGehee is a certified Mindful Self-Compassion (MSC) and Compassion for Couples (CfC) teacher and teacher-trainer, adjunct faculty at Seton Cove Spirituality Center, Austin, Texas, and has been a teaching and clinical professor in the Departments of Counseling Psychology and Clinical Psychology at the University of Texas, Austin.

website: mcgeheephd.com

Jarrett McGehee is a business owner and entrepreneur based in Austin, TX. Upon receiving his law degree, Jarrett began working in the legal and licensing departments of EMI/Capitol Records, Universal Music, and Mood Media where he negotiated and structured various music licensing agreements. During that time, he helped reissue and license the catalogs of many legendary artists including The Beatles, The Beach Boys, Frank Sinatra, and more. Jarrett recently founded *The Music Envoy* to advocate for creators by exploring and facilitating multiple revenue streams for its clients through copyright, licensing, and brand partnership initiatives.

website: musicenvoy.com

Printed in Great Britain
by Amazon

63038990R00078